One Kind Thing

Taylor Kennecartea   Illustrated by Ferlina Gunawan

For Ryan and Cora,
Always remember that kindness is the brightest light in this
world. Hold it close and keep it with care. I love you always.

Have you ever had a day where
every last thing feels crummy?

Where everything that happens
twists up and knots your tummy?

Some days are good,

some days are bad,

some days are just so-so

But there is one thing
you could do any day,
One thing that you should know.

The one thing is a kind thing,
A thing that makes a smile.
A kind thing is a great thing,
That can grow and lasts a while.

A kind thing can be any thing,
Like picking up some litter.

It can even be hugging a friend,
To make their day sweet instead of bitter.

The best thing about a kind thing,
is that it grows and grows.

Like a candle lighting a candle,
the kindness glows and glows.

Something about a kind thing

Makes the world a better place.

Maybe it's the warm fuzzy feeling.
Or the grin it puts on your face.

A kind thing is for everything,
for beings big

... or small.

A kind thing is an important thing.
We need it most of all.

Whatever it is, it's a magic thing.
What more is there to say?

A kind thing is a special thing.
What kind thing did you do today?

Author

Taylor lives in the mountains of California with their family and their many furry and feathered friends. Taylor writes stories for children, young adults, and grown ups, too.

Illustrator

Ferlina lives in small city in Indonesia. She likes to draw since childhood. In the meantime, she likes to nap and care for her succulents.